# The Painting Table

## A Journal of Loss and Joy

# ROGER HUTCHISON

Morehouse Publishing
NEW YORK · HARRISBURG · DENVER

Morehouse Publishing, 4785 Linglestown Road, Suite 101, Harrisburg, PA 17112
Morehouse Publishing, 19 East 34th Street, New York, NY 10016
Morehouse Publishing is an imprint of Church Publishing Incorporated.
www.churchpublishing.org

Cover art: Welcome Home (2011) by Roger Hutchison
Cover design by Laurie Klein Westhafer
Interior design and typesetting by Beth Oberholtzer

**Library of Congress Cataloging-in-Publication Data**
A catalog record of this book is available from the Library of Congress.

ISBN-13: 978-0-8192-2905-2 (pbk.)

*Printed in the United States of America*

For Mammaw

Melva Curry
September 16, 1916–February 18, 2004

*I sure do miss you.*

# Contents

# Acknowledgments

Sharon Pearson . . . my editor, and more importantly, my friend
*Your encouragement, love for, and support of The Painting Table means the world to me. Thank you.*

The children and families of Trinity Episcopal Cathedral, Columbia, South Carolina
*You bless my life every day. You've taught me to listen with my ears and listen with my heart.*

The children and families of Trinity Episcopal Church, Newtown, Connecticut
*I will never forget sharing The Painting Table with you. Your strength, resiliency, and smiles inspire me. Your light shines bright in the darkness.*

Riley Elizabeth
*I love being your dad. You are my greatest inspiration and joy.*

Kristin . . . my wife and best friend
*Thank you for the love and laughter. This is a pretty incredible life we are leading. I am so glad I share it with you. I can't wait to see what's next.*

# Foreword by Sandy Eisenberg Sasso

From one generation to the next we pass on bits of our lives, little by little, with words as simple as—"Don't be afraid. I am with you." We share parts of ourselves with actions as common as breaking bread and blowing on hot soup. Smiles and tears make imprints on our minds. Every encounter changes us.

The Native American poet, Joy Harjo, writes, "The world begins at the kitchen table." And perhaps it does. Under the table, pets nip at our ankles begging for food. It is here that babies bang their utensils and spill milk, where children play hide and seek, where they first taste sweet watermelon and spit out the seeds and learn manners, where adults light candles and place vases of flowers. It is here where families share the day, sometimes laugh, sometimes argue. It is at the table that we slam down our spoons in anger, pretend we are not hungry and walk away. It is here that we always return and offer thanks.

Loss and sorrow enter our homes and it is at the kitchen table that we take a deep breath and sit down. People tell us we have to eat; we have to let go even as we hold on. And we do what is required; we take the first bite—we share hard-boiled eggs, a sign that life, though different, continues. We prepare the food our dear ones once made or adored and our senses conjure up their presence.

There are nicks, scratches, and daps of color on our tables, the signs of crayons and paints gone astray. Another generation comes and suggests that we might want to buy a more contemporary table, or at the very least refurbish the old. But we won't, because every scratch and dent contains a memory.

And that is when it begins, the storytelling. The people who once gathered around that table are no more. Those who did Sunday crossword puzzles, those who quilted, and those who painted are gone. The conversations, the heated and the quiet ones, have been silenced. The dead feel no more pain; they don't weep anymore, but they don't laugh either.

It feels for a moment like nothing remains. But although it seems impossible, we discover that we can make something out of nothing. We can tell our loved one's story as it intertwines with ours. We can give that story voice as we color their lives with pen or brush. New generations watch and listen, and the past becomes part of who they are. It becomes part of their story.

Research teaches us that families who tell their children stories of their lives and help them tell their own stories, are more resilient. Young people come to realize that they are part of something bigger than themselves. They are part of a story that reaches back in time and they are connected to others in ways that are unique to them. Marshall Duke of Emory University calls those family narratives, our "fingerprint."

Roger Hutchison invites us to pull up a comfortable chair to his kitchen painting table and begin to write, to draw, to mark it with our fingerprint.

Rabbi Sandy Eisenberg Sasso is an award-winning author of many children's books including *God's Paintbrush* and *Creation's First Light* as well as *Midrash—Reading the Bible with Question Marks,* a book for adults.

# Introduction

As the Canon for Children's Ministries at Trinity Episcopal Cathedral in Columbia, South Carolina, I have the opportunity of leading weekly chapel services for the children of the Trinity Learning Center. These are grace-filled moments. We experience the stories of our faith through word, song, movement, and prayer. There is a palpable joy that fills the chapel when we gather together.

It is a thin and holy space where God is known.

Whether it is the call of the playground or simply a wandering mind, the children are sometimes unable to focus and it takes me a few moments to round them back in. This never happens to us adults, right?

"Listen with your ears . . . and listen with your heart." This is the mantra we speak when all focus seems lost. The children have come to love these words—and they say them with me—our voices fill the room with gladness and light.

Children understand what it means to listen with their hearts.

The poet, Mary Oliver, uses similar words in her poem "Sometimes" from *Red Bird: Poems* (Boston: Beacon Press, 2008):

> "Instructions for living a life.
> Pay attention.
> Be astonished.
> Tell about it."

I am an artist. I find joy when I move my paint-covered fingers across a blank canvas that sits atop my painting table. This is the place where I go to pray. This is the place where I go to listen with my heart. This is the place where the fullness of my life settles down and I can "pay attention" to that still small voice.

This simple book shares the familiar story of a boy, his grandmother, and the table where his earliest memories of love, commitment, and garden-grown tomatoes were served.

It is also an invitation to join me at my painting table. There are many different ways that you can use this book. Grieving the loss of a loved one, struggling in a relationship, or facing a major change in your life? This book is for you. Celebrating the birth of a child, entering a new phase of life, or just needing to be in community with others? This book is for you.

You are also invited to create your own Painting Table group in your church, school, or community for children and adults of all ages and abilities. The end result of The Painting Table is not the painting that is created. It is the conversation, sharing, and listening that takes place around the table. It is one mother comforting another mother as they both grieve for their friend who lost a child. It is like the conversation I had once with a third grade girl who told me she had had a really bad day. Her painting was dark and frantic. I listened to her for a little while—then encouraged her to paint another one. The second painting was a bit more colorful. She took her two paintings and smashed them together. When she pulled them apart, the darkness had lifted. I could see light, love, and a beautiful smile.

And sometimes the Painting Table helps us express our gratitude for life, as well. We are created in God's image so at the very center of our being is that need and desire to create. One does not have to be a "trained" or "professional" artist to do this. Have you ever watched a child coloring or painting? There is an authenticity and holy joy in that very moment. Resources for starting your own Painting Table group can be found within these pages. You can also find more at www.thepaintingtable.com

While there is grief, sadness, and loss, there is also hope. There is an opportunity for celebration as we gather together, break bread, talk, and are welcomed. Whether through cooking, painting, or Eucharist, we come together to remember.

For many, life happens around the kitchen table, but here we gather at the painting table where you are invited to draw pictures, record memories, and experience transformation and new birth through the creation of something original within the pages of this book. There are pages in this book set aside just for this.

I encourage you to listen with your ears . . . and listen with your heart . . . then tell us all about it!

I've been waiting for you. I receive you with open arms as my Grandmother did and God does. Let us break bread together.

Thank you for joining me. I am glad you are here.

Roger Hutchison
June 2013

# THE PAINTING TABLE
## Story

Life happened around the

# kitchen table.

It was a simple oak table adorned with plain dishes and a bounty of fresh fruits and vegetables.

There were

### tomatoes and squash,
### okra and peas.

The colors of the food, fresh and jewel-like, made the table shine like a rainbow.

There was no silver. There was no pretense.

Excited and eager conversation moved around the table like smooth river stones being skipped across the glassy surface of a pond.

## We held hands.

We held our breaths.

We offered thanksgiving; we broke bread.

I never wanted it to end.

I received the table

as a gift

when my Mammaw died.

It is the same simple oak table

where laughter,

love, and gifts from the garden

gave us life.

It was the same table, when covered with quilts and blankets,

that made the best fort.

It is the same table where the hospice nurse told us

the end

of Mammaw's life

was near.

# I miss her.

Her laughing eyes. Her servant's heart.

I miss her hands and I miss her hugs.

I miss her silly and often irreverent sense of humor.

I miss the once-a-week trips to the grocery store.

I miss picking berries with her.

I miss the fishing trips we would take together—a boy and his

Grandmother—cane poles and wiggling worms.


I miss the sound of her voice reading to my Pappaw. I would sneak

out, after bedtime. I would lie down in the hallway with my face

pressed to the floor, and

## listen to the stories she would tell.

I have a picture of her next to my bed.

She is holding our daughter, Riley.

It was the first and only time they ever met.

A curious baby girl and her proud Great-Grandmother.

It is the last thing I see when I go to bed each night and the first thing

I see each morning.

It is one of our most cherished possessions.

The table is still covered with the colors of ripe tomatoes and okra—

of blackberry cobbler and yellow squash.

Conversation and confession still echo around the table,

but only I can hear it now.

# I am an artist and the table is where I paint.

It is my painting table.

There are reds and yellows, purples and browns—a rainbow

of colors spread out across its surface. It is the place where

I share my deepest thoughts and imaginings.

It is the place where I go to pray.

It is the place where I go to remember.

Friend, will you join me at my painting table?

There are stories to tell.

# THE PAINTING TABLE
## Journal

# How to Use This Book

The journal component of this book is designed for both writing and sketching. Through the story of The Painting Table, the different paintings in the book, and the different heading words and quotes included in the journal section of this book, I hope you will be inspired to open your heart and soul to the benefits of personal reflection through word and art. Use this book as a tool to help facilitate this process.

Whether you choose to keep this journal as a way to look back at spiritual events that took place in your life at any given time, as a way to record answered prayers, or as a reminder of individuals and situations that require inclusion in your prayers—it makes no difference. It is up to you.

Small groups such as grief groups or Confirmation classes can also use this book and journal as a way to explore writing and painting as prayer. Choose whatever you would like to write or draw with: pencil, pen, marker, crayon, or pastels. If you would like to use paint—tempera or watercolor—you may choose to purchase appropriate paper at any store that has art supplies. Create your own painting table. Again, it is up to you.

# Remember

*"And when your sorrow is comforted (time soothes all sorrows) you will be content that you have known me. You will always be my friend."* —Antoine de Saint-Exupery

# Prayer

*I thank my God every time I remember you, constantly praying with joy in every one of my prayers for all of you.*
—*Philippians 1:3–4*

# Hope

*"Be faithful in small things because it is in them that your strength lies."* —Mother Teresa

# Fear

*"No one ever told me that grief felt so like fear."* —C. S. Lewis

# Joy

*"It's wonderful to climb the liquid mountains of the sky. Behind me and before me is God and I have no fears."* —Helen Keller

# Peace

*"Come to me, all you that are weary and are carrying heavy burdens, and I will give you rest. Take my yoke upon you, and learn from me; for I am gentle and humble in heart, and you will find rest for your souls. For my yoke is easy, and my burden is light."* —*Matthew 11:28–30*

# Quiet

*"Everything has its wonders, even darkness and silence,
and I learn whatever state I am in, therein to be content."*
—Helen Keller

# Healing

*"When we honestly ask ourselves which person in our lives means the most to us, we often find that it is those who, instead of giving advice, solutions, or cures, have chosen rather to share our pain and touch our wounds with a warm and tender hand."*
—Henri Nouwen

# Community

*"What should young people do with their lives today? Many things, obviously. But the most daring thing is to create stable communities in which the terrible disease of loneliness can be cured." —Kurt Vonnegut*

# Love

*Beloved, let us love one another, because love is from God;*
*everyone who loves is born of God and knows God.*
*—1 John 4:7*

# How to Form a Painting Table Group

My painting table is an actual table, but the idea of the Painting Table is more than a wooden top with four legs. It is about the invitation. It is about our sharing our own sacred stories. It is a safe and holy space where conversation, prayer, and healing can take place. The canvas, paper, and other assorted art supplies are the simple tools that help bring us together.

You do not need any artistic experience or training to be a part of the Painting Table. It is not about what your final creation looks like. It is about the transformation that takes place when you sit with others around a table for a period of time—creating, sharing, dreaming, and praying—together. And it can certainly be done in solitude, all by yourself.

It is about what happens in your heart and in your soul.

## Planning a Painting Table Group

In starting a Painting Table group, you will need to have a clear vision on who will be invited to participate. Is this a children's group? Is this a group for individuals journeying through grief and loss? Is this a group for those with special needs? Is this a group of new mothers or fathers? There is not a limit to how the Painting Table can be used.

The length of a Painting Table group can vary. I have facilitated groups that met one time and I have led groups that meet once a week for several weeks. Lenten groups are especially powerful.

Choosing a meeting space for your group is very important. An ideal room would fit the size of your group—not too small where you are bumping into each other, and not so cavernous that your group feels lost.

It would be ideal if the room had a sink or was near a kitchen or restroom.

*Some of the materials I have used include:*
- Newspaper or plastic table cloths to cover the tables
- Assorted papers/canvas that can be used for drawing, watercolor, or painting
- Pencils
- Watercolors

- Acrylic or Tempera paints (Be aware that unless the container says washable, the paints will stain.)
- Crayons and colored pencils
- Oil or chalk pastels
- Assortment of paintbrushes (I paint with my hands—you can too!)
- Paper towels and baby wipes

## Leading a Painting Table Group

What happens during an actual Painting Table session is completely up to you. In my opinion, the less structured the better. I like to open with a prayer. I also include the lighting of a candle. A burning candle is a wonderfully simple way to acknowledge the presence of God in the space and in the group that has gathered. The candle is extinguished at the end of the meeting after the closing prayer.

Once the session has been opened with prayer, offer a few words of encouragement, especially for those who are beginners or have anxiety about their "artistic" skills. Remember, this is not about the final product. Remind people that whatever is discussed or shared within the group remains in the group. Groups such as these tend to get extremely personal when meeting over a period of weeks.

Gathering for the Painting Table is a simple and holy exercise. Enter into it with humility, openness, and trust.

Lastly, have fun and enjoy this leg of the journey!

About the Paintings

I approach painting as a form of prayer. I sit at my painting table for a while in silence—listening for that "still small voice." I then begin to select my colors and enter into the process of translating my prayers into paintings. I never know what the outcome will be.

I am not a professionally trained artist. I did take a class or two in college, but I am mostly self-taught. I had tried painting with brushes, but they got in the way. In listening for that "still small voice," I found my passion. Now I paint with my hands.

Simply put—I cherish the life I have been given and I searched a long time for a way to say thank you. When I sit at the painting table, I find that I am able to do this in a way that can only be described as holy.

It is my hope that the paintings included in this book inspire and encourage you to be open to healing and joy in your life.

*Welcome Home* (cover, page 11), 16x20, Acrylic on Canvas, 2011
This painting features my Mammaw's little home—or any home where we feel safe and loved.

*Kindred* (page 13), 24x24, Acrylic on Canvas, 2013
I have always used circles to represent God. The large circle represents God and the two small circles represent man and woman—made in the image of God.

*Abundance* (page 15), 20x24, Acrylic on Canvas, 2011
This painting is filled with many colors and circles. There is a fullness and abundance. It reminds me of what my Mammaw's table looked like covered in vegetables.

*Balance* (page 17), 30x40, Acrylic on Canvas, 2012
The image really speaks for itself. I love the beauty of stacked stones. It speaks to the balance of life that we all seek to find.

*Seasons* (page 19), 20x20, Acrylic on Canvas, 2011

The sky and water are joined together—it looks almost like a chalice. The water seems to pour forth from the bowl of the chalice. The colorful circles represent transition, seasons, life . . . and death. From dust to dust . . .

*Childhood* (page 21), 20x24, Acrylic on Canvas, 2012

There are three components to this painting. The tree represents life. The tire swing represents the joys of childhood. The stars in the tree's branches represent the wishes and dreams of a young child or a child at heart.

*Spirit Wind* (page 23), 36x36, Acrylic on Canvas, 2011

This painting represents the presence of God in the swirling dance we call life.

*Turbulent Night Sky* (page 25), 24x24, Acrylic on Canvas, 2012

I love a star-filled night sky—a place where we all seem to focus our hopes and dreams. It can also be a place of loneliness and despair. The fullness of the moon speaks to God's presence. This painting now lives in the home of a friend whose young daughter, Hudson, left this life far too soon.

*Prayer* (title page, page 29), 12x12, Acrylic on Canvas, 2012

This small painting speaks to the power of prayer and of remembering.

*Genesis* (page 31), 36x36, Acrylic on Canvas, 2012

This vibrant painting speaks to Creation. It also speaks to the seasons and beauty of life.

*In Retrospect* (page 33), 30x40, Acrylic on Canvas, 2012

We all have a story to tell. This painting features three "windows" that focus on three different stories. One window draws the eye toward a turbulent waterscape. Another window draws your eye toward a cold and dark winter scene. The final window features a green and peaceful landscape.

# About the Author and Artist

When Roger felt the need to express his relationship with God, he turned to painting. At first, painting traditionally (with brushes) just didn't trip the tumblers to unlock what was inside him that he wanted to transfer to the canvas. So one night, he put aside the brushes and put his hands directly into his medium. This visceral act enabled him to tap directly into his heart and mind, creating works described as "a collective dream, common to us all," and "wonderfully introspective . . . as if he is having a conversation with each piece as it is coming together."

Roger says, "Painting is the way I talk to God. I find joy when I move my fingers through puddles of color and across blank canvas. I am always surprised—and blessed—by the conversation that takes place. It is as if a good friend has joined me for a glass of wine and time of catching up. I invite you to pull up a chair . . . let's talk."

In addition to his calling at Trinity Episcopal Cathedral (Columbia, South Carolina) ministering to children from age three through the fifth grade, Roger has burst onto the local art scene showing his works at Piccolo Spoleto, Columbia Museum of Art, South Carolina State Museum, Main Street's Frame of Mind, Verve, Mr. Friendly's, and Tombo Grille. He has become a favorite of local designers, and collectors hail from as far away as New York and Australia.

Roger also enjoys creative writing, photography, and gardening. Most of all, Roger enjoys spending time with his wife Kristin, daughter Riley (11), and their cockapoo, Scout. Roger received his undergraduate degree from Warren Wilson College in Asheville, North Carolina, and has completed some master's level work at Virginia Theological Seminary in Alexandria, Virginia.

Roger's website www.thepaintingtable.com features his paintings, his reflections, and experiences with The Painting Table.

William Thrift wrote a portion of this biography for a feature article published in *Columbia Home and Garden Magazine* in 2012. Used with permission.